Plan B

a gift for

Mark "9/4/2012"

from

Mom + Ray

I know the plans I have for you,

declares the Lord,

plans to prosper you and not to harm you,

plans to give you hope and a future.

Jeremiah 29:11

Published by Hallmark Books,
a division of Hallmark Cards, Inc.,
Kansas City, MO 64141
Visit us on the web at www.Hallmark.com.

Unless otherwise identified, scripture quotations are from THE HOLY BIBLE, NEW INTERNATIONAL VERSION®.
Copyright 1973, 1978, 1984 by International Bible Society. Used by permission of Zondervan Publishing
House. All rights reserved.

Scripture quotations identified KJV are from the King James Version of the Bible.

Scripture quotations marked NCV are taken from The Holy Bible, New Century Version, copyright 1987,
1988, 1991 by Word Publishing, Dallas, Texas 75039. Used by permission.

Scripture quotations identified RSV are from the Revised Standard Version of the Bible. Copyright 1946,
1952, 1971 by the Division of Christian Education of the National Council of Churches of Christ in the
USA. Used by permission.

Scripture quotations identified NKJV are from the New King James Version of the Bible, copyright 1979,
1980, 1982 by Thomas Nelson, Inc. Used by permission. All rights reserved.

Scripture quotations marked NLT are taken from the Holy Bible, New Living Translation, copyright 1996.
Used by permission of Tyndale House Publishers, Inc., Wheaton, Illinois 60189. All rights reserved.

Scripture quotations identified NASB are taken from the New American Standard Bible, copyright The
Lockman Foundation 1960, 1962, 1963, 1968, 1971, 1972, 1973, 1975, 1977, 1995. Used by permission.

Scripture quotations marked TLB are taken from The Living Bible © 1971. Used by permission of Tyndale
House Publishers, Inc., Wheaton, Illinois 60189. All rights reserved.

Scripture quotations marked MSG are taken from THE MESSAGE. Copyright 1993, 1994, 1995, 1996, 2000,
2001, 2002. Used by permission of NavPress Publishing Group.

Scripture quotations marked CEV are taken from the Contemporary English Version of the Bible,
copyright © 1995 by American Bible Society.

Editorial Director: Todd Hafer
Art Director: Kevin Swanson
Designer: Myra Colbert Advertising & Design: Myra Colbert, Kevin Marozas
Production Artist: Dan C. Horton

Editorial development by Scott Degelman & Associates.

ISBN: 978-1-59530-174-1

BOK3092

Printed and bound in China

Hallmark
GIFT BOOKS

God

always

has

a

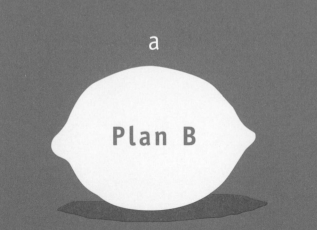

Plan B

Introduction

"When one door closes, another opens."
— Alexander Graham Bell

God possesses some amazing powers: parting seas, magically providing food from heaven, raising the dead.

But one of our Creator's more underrated powers is His ability to turn stumbling blocks into stepping stones. That's what this book is all about. One door of opportunity closes, but God opens another one. A failure mysteriously evolves into the key for success down the road. Bitter rejection becomes the fuel for a new level of focus and determination. It's all about the Bible's promise that "in all things God works for the good of those who love him." (Romans 8:28)

As you'll read in *God Always Has a Plan B*, this promise doesn't mean that everything that happens to us is good. It does mean, however, that God can take the ugly things life hurls at us and somehow make them beautiful. He can bring us through the worst of times and make us stronger, more hopeful, and more grateful people in the process.

Whatever your life challenges may be, our prayer is that this book will help you discover a loving God's Plan B just for you.

Bless you, and thank you for reading.

Scott Degelman and Friends

God has a **Plan B**

for being there just when you need Him

"No problem is so big that it won't fit in God's hands."

– Suzanne Berry

Are there certain people in your life who you are sure are against you? A co-worker, a neighbor, or even a family member?

If you suspect this is the case – even if you are sure this is the case – take heart! Because God is for you! He's on your side. All the time. And "all the time" includes right now. God is thinking about you, loving you, and supporting you, even as you read these words. How cool is that?

God is not a fair-weather being. He doesn't offer His love and comfort to you only when you are doing everything right and your attitude toward Him is perfect. You don't have to earn your Heavenly Father's loyalty – and you won't lose it just because you make a mistake. You have been created with a purpose in life – a purpose uniquely suited to your talents and temperament. And God is committed to seeing you fulfill that purpose. He isn't watching you from on high, hoping to see you fail. He's right beside you, cheering you on, comforting you through failure, encouraging you through adversity.

Life can be tough sometimes, and if people in your life occasionally become your rivals, that can make things just that much tougher. But remember always that no matter who your opponent is, you can't be defeated. That's because God is for you, and with Him in your corner, cheering you on and instructing you, you will ultimately have your hand raised in victory.

Always remember: Because God is for you, it doesn't really matter who might be against you!

**The Lord will
guide you always;
he will satisfy
your needs.**
Isaiah 58:11

God has a **Plan B**

for facing fear

"The Lord stands above the new day,
for God has made it.
All restlessness, all worry, and anxiety
flee before him."
– Dietrich Bonhoeffer

Katie Brown weighs only 95 pounds, and she is just a bit over 5 feet tall. She stands a lot taller than that, however, once she's nimbly scaled a 100-foot climbing wall. (That's equivalent to a 10-story building.)

Katie is a "difficulty climber," an endeavor in which she's a world champion and multiple gold medalist at the X Games, which you may have seen televised on networks like ESPN2.

As you might imagine, it's intimidating for a small person to attack climbing walls and cliffs that are 20 times her height, but Katie says that extreme faith can bring her peace, even in extremely dangerous challenges. "I know that I couldn't have done what I've done without being a Christian," she explains. "My faith in God doesn't get rid of my healthy fear of climbing extreme heights, but it does help me deal with it. It takes away a lot of the pressure, because you know that God's not going to condemn you if you don't win. So there's nothing to worry about. When I see others competing, I wonder how I could compete if I didn't have faith in God."

The "walls" you face in your life might not be literal or physical. They might be emotional or relational. And it's OK to feel intimidated or frightened by those walls. As Katie notes, it would be unhealthy not to appreciate the significance of a major challenge.

But, like Katie, you can rest secure in the truth that God will not condemn you if you can't get to the top of your wall – or if it takes you hundreds of attempts. God is more concerned in your faithful effort.

God is our refuge and strength.

Psalm 46:1 KJV

God has a **Plan B**

for providing rest for the weary

"First, keep peace within yourself;
then you can also bring peace to others."
— Thomas à Kempis

If you read the Bible, you'll find a lot of physical imagery used to explain God — even though He is a spirit and is beyond flesh and bones. But, in order to help us flesh-and-bone folk understand our Creator, the biblical writers talk about God's hands, His eyes, even His wings.

But you won't find a single verse using this image: the sweat glands of God. That's because God doesn't sweat. He doesn't get tired or suffer from aching muscles. He never gets stressed out, despite the size of a task. He doesn't enter his mansion after a hard millennium's work and say, "Whew-boy, I sure could use a hot shower, a couple Advil, and a mentholated rubdown from an angel!"

God is superhuman, tireless, and all-powerful. Yet what did He do after creating the world? He rested. Let that sink into your brain. God. Rested. He didn't need to rest, but He purposefully took the time to step back, cease working, and enjoy His creation. If an all-powerful being made time to rest, that should speak volumes to us mere mortals.

As a member of the human race, you need to rest occasionally. You need to focus on "human," once in a while, and not so much on "race." You need to take time to recover physically, emotionally, and spiritually from life's demands. You need time to take stock of where you've been, where you are, and where you are headed. You need quiet, reflective, and restful moments – away from stress and to-do lists. You need to take the time to be a friend, a parent, a child of God.

It's possible to become so obsessed with work, finances, or familial obligations that you ignore your body's physical and mental signals that rest and replenishment are needed. It's not wise to disregard those signals. Various studies – including a recent one at the University of Chicago – reveal that those who fail to recharge their mental and physical batteries once in a while are more susceptible to illness and stress-related problems such as ulcers – and to mistakes on the job. Rest can help you avoid such perils.

Additionally, in resting, you will find the time and the right frame of mind to contemplate God's wonders and to thank Him for His grace and kindness to you. And you can gather the energy to live your life to the fullest.

There's no question – you need rest to be at your best. But rest can be elusive. How can you fit some down-time into an already-crowded life?

Here are a few tips:

First, build rest time into your daily schedule. Let's face it, if you're like many people, that's the only way you'll refrain from non-stop work and activity. And it's OK to be a bit selfish, a bit inflexible about this rest time. If you aren't, something else will crowd it out. Take a regular 20-minute walk after lunch or at mid-afternoon break time. A growing trend among businesspeople is to head for the car every afternoon, recline the seat, and grab a 15-minute power nap.

Second, use your vacation time. All of it. If you're self-employed, give yourself at least a couple of weeks off each year. And go someplace for vacation, even if it's just to a nearby town. If you don't "get out of Dodge," you might find yourself being pulled back into the job. One executive at a large U.S. company makes a point of scheduling vacations in remote areas, where he will be almost impossible to reach – even by cell phone.

Another great way to take a load off is to pursue interests and hobbies that differ from what you do on the job. And, in this case, adopting a favorite TV show can count as an "interest." This strategy can help you engage and feed your brain and body in a way that your job does not. At the same time, it will give those often-used job-related parts a needed respite.

Finally, get adequate sleep at night. Your body needs it. Your mind needs it. Sure, you might be able to get more work done if you sleep fewer hours a night, but at what cost?

To be at your best, to be healthy, to be a well-rounded person, to fully and truly enjoy life, you must find the time to rest your body, mind, and spirit. Think of all the beyond-the-call-of-duty hours you spend working. Think of what that time could mean to your family, your well-being, and your relationship with God — the God who understands the value of occasional rest time.

> Come to me, all you who are
> weary and burdened,
> and I will give you rest.
>
> Matthew 11:28

God has a **Plan B**

for timing and circumstances

"Troubles are often the tools by which
God fashions us for better things."

– Henry Ward Beecher

A man named Wayne Dyer wrote a book that he believed would touch the lives of thousands of readers. He sent his finished manuscript to many publishers – and got back nothing but rejection letters. Not one saw any market for Dyer's work.

Discouraged but undaunted, he dipped into his own pocket and published the book himself. Then he hit the road to peddle it. He arranged appearances on local talk shows around the country, then stuffed his car full of books. In each city, he informed local booksellers that he was going to be interviewed on radio or TV, offering to provide books to meet the demand.

Dyer kept at it for two years, selling a handful of books in city after city. Still, no publisher would take a chance on this unknown author.

One night, he taped a 3 a.m. TV show in San Francisco. He figured that no more than a couple dozen insomniacs would be watching. But one of those insomniacs was Johnny Carson, host of The Tonight Show. Carson liked what he saw. Dyer got booked on the show. Sales of the book, *Your Erroneous Zones*, skyrocketed, and Dyer became a best-selling author, and eventually, host of his own TV series.

The lesson here? Don't give up on something you believe in – even if the initial reaction is less than what you hope for. Keep giving it your best. You never know who might be listening or watching or reading.

Work hard so God can say to you, "Well done."

2 Timothy 2:15 TLB

God has a **Plan B**

for comfort in uncertain times

"In the darkest part of the forest,
the spirit shines brightest."

— Lauren Benson

Have you ever tried to explain a complex subject or philosophical axiom to a child? It can be frustrating. Sometimes small children just don't seem to understand what their elders are telling them – especially when it comes to answering that never-ending little-kid question, "Why?"

In our information-rich world, we have figured out so much, unraveled so many of life's tangled mysteries. But there is much more that we don't understand. And, just like a child who can't understand why she can't touch the moon – or why he can't eat candy for every meal –

we question God about things that don't make sense to us. We demand to know "why" when life doesn't go according to our plan. At times like these, we forget that all that we know (or think we know) is a tiny droplet in the vast ocean of God's knowledge.

The Bible reminds us that God's ways are much higher than our ways, and we can comprehend only tiny shreds of His comprehensive master plan. Our responsibility is to follow Him, and everything will ultimately work out for good. This doesn't mean that everything that happens in life is good. But it does mean that even the most frightening, terrible stories can have happy endings when we place our trust in God and strive to obey Him.

So, learn to appreciate life's questions. You can learn much about yourself – and about life itself – from the questions that emerge day to day. And remember that God, the Master Architect of the Universe, has chosen to reach beyond the sun, the moon, and the stars to take your hand. The road ahead of you might be completely unfamiliar and intimidating. You might not know where the road will ultimately lead. But if you travel it hand in hand with God, your journey and your destination will be truly rewarding.

You might be walking, even stumbling, along a rocky life-path right now. But the terrain underneath you and the uncharted territory ahead of you pale in comparison to the loving, powerful God who walks beside you.

> **As the heavens are higher than the earth,**
> **so are my ways higher than your ways**
> **and my thoughts than your thoughts.**
>
> Isaiah 55:9

God has a **Plan B**

for true contentment

"We are not here to be successful.
We are here to be faithful."

– Mother Teresa

What's on your life's wish list right now? What do you wish you had, but don't possess? For many, money and material possessions top the list. Americans have a possession obsession: We want bigger, better TVs, faster computers, and MP3s with more memory and longer battery life.

For others, status and success are the ultimate prize. Some want to be the next pop star, game show champion, or winner of a new face and better body.

Seeking "the good life" isn't inherently bad – as long as this quest is secondary to "the God life." Unfortunately, the drives for material possessions and physical attractiveness can become all-consuming goals – a shallow, self-gratifying obsession with no eternal significance.

God's Word teaches us to travel light. In fact, Jesus instructed His followers to take with them only the bare necessities when they set out on a journey. He reminded them not to be distracted by the glitter of money or the aura of fame and power.

In truth, the light of God's divine love is so brilliant that it makes everything else dull in comparison. God's light is the one we should run to, because only in that light can we find true happiness and fulfillment. So don't misplace your hope in things that have no lasting value. Put loving and serving God atop your list of life's priorities. Because, of all the treasures life has to offer, God tops them all.

The world and its desires

pass away,

but the man who does

the will of God lives forever.

1 John 2:17

God has a **Plan B**

for "rocking what you got"

"God's gifts put man's best dreams to shame."

– Elizabeth Barrett Browning

Imagine receiving a gift from a wealthy person who is renowned for her taste in selecting perfect (and expensive) presents for everyone on her gift list. Wouldn't this be a package you would be eager to open? A gift you would want to start enjoying right away?

Sadly, many people have received gifts from the perfect Giver, but they never bother to open them or use them for their intended purpose. "This is nice," they say, "but I was really hoping for something else."

God has gifted each of us with abilities. And he never makes a mistake. His gifts are never the wrong size or style – or inappropriate in any way. No one has ever needed to return a gift from God.

If only we will open God's heaven-sent gifts, we can use them in a way that will benefit others and bring glory to Him. Do you know what your gifts are? (A sense of humor, a talent for art, the ability to encourage others? – just to name a few.) Are you using your gifts? Or are they lying dormant, gathering dust? If this is the case, it's time to tear into that aging wrapping paper.

Putting your God-given talents to work is one of the most satisfying things you will ever do. As you do what God created you for, you gain a deep sense of purpose and become closer and more grateful to the One who gave you your talents. Few things are as beautiful as Creator and creation working together. So don't neglect your gifts. Don't wish you had someone else's. Do all the good you can with what you've been given.

**Every good and perfect gift is from above,
coming down from the Father of the heavenly lights.**

James 1:17

God has a **Plan B**

for inner peace

**"Even if the whole world doubts, believe anyway.
With God all things are possible."**

– Paige DeRuyscher

If you're a fan of TV's nature channels, you might have seen the footage of the anaconda who captured an unfortunate deer. The deer struggled to escape, but every time it moved, it merely allowed the anaconda's coils to tighten, slowly squeezing the life from another cousin of Bambi. Soon, the deer was lunch.

Worry can be like that anaconda. Your doubts about your own abilities, your uncertainty about others' feelings toward you, your anxieties about what might happen in the future – they become like reptilian coils that surround you and squeeze the energy and hope out of you. And the more you struggle against them, the tighter those coils constrict.

Want to avoid the crushing, oppressive power of The Worry Snake? Want to keep your anxieties from dominating your life? You have two weapons at your disposal: The first is perspective; the other is peace. Think of them as two clubs you can use to beat that worrisome snake on the head when it slithers up to you.

The apostle Paul, who wrote much of the Bible's New Testament, was a man who possessed perspective. He instructed fellow believers to be "anxious for nothing." Think about those words. Paul says we shouldn't worry about anything. And he didn't give this advice flippantly. He was in prison when he wrote it. In fact, he spent lots of time in various dirtbag dungeons, where he was beaten, clamped in chains, and separated from those he loved.

Beyond these trials, Paul had some type of "thorn in the flesh," a physical condition that pained him so much that he asked God repeatedly to cure him. God, in this case, said no.

When he wasn't in jail, Paul was getting shipwrecked, bitten by a poisonous snake, and pelted with stones by people who didn't appreciate his outspoken faith. Ultimately, his belief in God got him beheaded.

So, when a guy like this tells us not to worry, we should listen. And we should emulate the kind of perspective he had. Paul knew what was truly important. He knew God loved him and had a plan for his life.

God loves you, too. He has a plan for your life. And that plan doesn't include being consumed by worry. So maintain the right perspective. Will the world stop turning if you don't climb to the top of the corporate ladder or become a world-famous entertainer? Will babies no longer giggle and birds no longer sing if you don't make a million dollars – or you don't lose the 10 pounds you hope to shed this year? What is a traffic ticket or flat tire or late assignment or cold sore compared with being loved purely and eternally by Almighty God and being made clean from all of your sins?

Paul operated his life from this kind of heavenly perspective – a perspective that gave him peace (there's your Club No. 2), despite all the painful trials he endured.

Paul learned a key truth about peace: God doesn't always untie all the knots in our lives, those things that make us worry. But, in these cases, the Heavenly Father does give His children the grace to live with the knots. And that divine grace brings peace.

So remember, there is nothing you face that is too difficult, too troubling, or too frightening for God. God doesn't have sweat glands, remember? Problems don't keep Him up at night – He's awake and on the job all of the time.

Use this knowledge of God's power to transform worry time into an opportunity to seek God's perspective and God's peace, the way Paul did.

When he was in jail, for example, instead of worrying about how he was being treated or when he would be released, he wrote letters of encouragement and instruction to people he knew – to large groups of believers and to individual friends. He sang hymns of praise to God.

In at least one case, he led his jailer to a saving faith. You can follow Paul's lead. If, for example, you and some of your friends fear getting laid off at work, don't spend your days and nights fretting over what might happen – and when it might happen to you. Do your best work. Determine a contingency plan in the event your jobs are eliminated. Help your friends develop action plans of their own. Be someone with whom they can share their fears and anxieties. Encourage one another. It's amazing how helping others can eliminate worry and stress.

And don't forget to tell God how you feel. Thank Him for all that He's given you, and seek His wisdom for your future.

God loves you. He cares about your life. And He is completely capable of carrying your worries. What a peaceful truth that is. So the next time you feel worry squeezing the life out of you, remember the words of Paul, the physically impaired, oft-jailed martyr:

"The Lord is near. Do not be anxious about anything, but in everything, by prayer and petition, with thanksgiving, present your requests to God. And the peace of God, which transcends all understanding, will guard your hearts and your minds in Christ Jesus." (Philippians 4:5-7)

Never forget that a peace that can transcend all understanding can certainly transcend worry, too.

Therefore do not worry about tomorrow,

for tomorrow will worry about itself.

Each day has enough trouble of its own.

Matthew 6:34

God has a **Plan B**

for fulfilling your
life's purpose

**"God made you as you are
in order to use you as He planned."**

— J. C. Macauley

What is your passion in life? What do you enjoy more than anything else in the world – the kind of thing you know you will never grow tired of? Maybe it's music, art, teaching others, or some type of creative writing. If you have found your passion, you know there is a sense of wonder about it.

Former professional baseball pitcher Dave Dravecky loved his sport so much that he confessed, "I would have played for nothin'."

And today, he brings that same kind of passion to his callings as a writer and head of a ministry for cancer victims and amputees.

What about you? Are you pursuing your passion? Sure, there are required duties at home, on the job, or at school. But what about the world beyond the must-dos? Are you participating in the activities or pursuits you truly love – or just the ones you think will make you more popular or look best on a resume? What are you doing to ignite your sense of wonder or challenge yourself? In other words, are you making the grade or making a difference? Are you following the crowd or following the call of your heart?

If much of your life is sheer drudgery, you might be missing God's purpose for you. Think of the first disciples Jesus called. They all left what they were doing to follow Him. Their hearts pounded with excitement and anticipation of the adventures ahead.

The Lord wants no less for you. His plan for you is to experience a vibrant life, in perfect harmony with the gifts He has given you. So don't let your life be a series of random events. Live it on purpose; live it with passion.

True happiness is knowing that you are constantly in the process of becoming what you were meant to be.

I have not yet reached my goal, and I am not perfect.
But Christ has taken hold of me. So I keep on running
and struggling to take hold of the prize.

Philippians 3:12 CEV

God has a **Plan B**

for drying our tears

"Without the rain, there would be no rainbow."

– G. K. Chesterton

When you were a small child, who did you run to when you fell down and hurt yourself? Who wiped away your tears when someone said something so cruel to you that you couldn't help but cry? Who was your refuge when, despite your best efforts, you didn't win the race, earn the A, or find the lost toy? Perhaps it was your mother or grandmother who was always handy with a tissue or a kind word. Or maybe it was your father or a big brother who lent you a handkerchief or brushed away your tears with a large but tender finger.

Writing in the book of Revelation, the Bible's grand finale, the apostle John promises that someday God Himself will wipe away your tears. Think about that for a moment: The same hands that stretched out the heavens, scattered the stars across the sky, and formed mountains will someday gently touch your cheeks and brush away your tears forever.

And when those final tears disappear, so will the fear, despair, and pain that accompanied them. One of the coolest things about heaven is that it's a place of perfect happiness. There will be room for friendship, worship, celebration, and joy.

But, as big as heaven is, it can't hold everything. There will simply be no room for tears. It's doubtful, though, that anyone will miss them. Whatever the sources of grief in your life right now, God wants to dry your tears. It would be a crying shame if you didn't let Him.

God will wipe away

every tear from their eyes.

Revelation 21:4 NKJV

God has a **Plan B**

for giving temptation
the cold shoulder

"A quiet conscience sleeps in thunder."

– English proverb

Ranchers have a saying: "Once you're tromping through a cow pasture, it's a little late to worry about soiling your Sunday shoes."

This bit of sound advice carries far beyond the ranch fences. The key to avoiding danger and sin is determining, in advance, to stay far away from compromising situations.

Be aware, however, that sometimes trouble will reveal itself a little bit at a time. It can pique your curiosity, beckoning you to come closer, "just for a look." The next thing you know, you're up to your knees in it.

Right now, promise God and yourself that you will resist giving temptation even a passing glance. Don't allow yourself to fantasize about indulging in some kind of sin. As singer Steven Curtis Chapman puts it (in a song titled "Run Away"), "Don't even look in the direction of a thought you should not entertain."

Another key to avoiding trouble is to prayerfully decide ahead of time how you will handle various unavoidable temptations – the ones you don't see coming until they're upon you. What will you say if some innocent flirtation starts to turn inappropriate? What will you do if some colleagues at work start cutting corners and expect you to go along for the ride – or at least keep silent about it?

To the best of your ability and knowledge, determine where the "cow pastures" are in your life, and decide how you're going to avoid them. There is trouble underfoot, so tread carefully. Don't step in something you shouldn't.

I've banked your promises
in the vault of my heart
so I won't sin myself bankrupt.

Psalm 119:11 MSG

God has a **Plan B**

for solving life's puzzles

"Trust God. Sounds corny, works every time."

– Ellen Brenneman

One of Colorado's many ski resorts offers its guests a challenge beyond those they might find on the slopes: a large maze. The maze is composed of row after row of shoulder-high walls, leading to one dead end after another. The maze is so complex that the resort offers a prize to anyone who can complete it within an allotted time limit.

Above the maze sits a dining area, where a person's friends or relatives can shout guidance for navigating the labyrinth: "You're going the wrong way – you'll never get through if you keep going that direction!" "Keep turning right, and you'll be OK!" "You need to backtrack; you're headed for a dead end!"

Of course, the people inside the maze don't particularly want to hear any advice. They think they can figure things out if they just trust their instincts and sense of direction. It almost never works. Others try to ask their fellow maze navigators for advice, but find that everyone inside the maze is, for the most part, equally lost and confused.

Finally, after the time limit has elapsed and the prize forfeited, the maze runners will look up forlornly for guidance from their family or friends, who have the better vantage point. They'll turn up their palms, shrug their shoulders, and say something like, "Where am I, and how do I get out of this place!?"

Many people today are like those lost souls in the maze. They think they can figure life out for themselves. They are too proud to seek help from someone with a better vantage point. But in reality, they are lost – and getting "loster."

God lives above the confusing labyrinth we deal with each day. His perspective is better than ours, and He sees exactly where we need to go and what we need to avoid. All we need to do is quit looking at the confusion in front of us and look to Him instead.

If we'll surrender our will, God will show us the way.

> **Thy word is a lamp unto my feet,**
> **and a light unto my path.**
> **Psalm 119:105 KJV**

God has a **Plan B**

for blessing His peacemakers

"In life, just as in music,
harmony makes life beautiful."

- Olivia Kent

If you were given millions of dollars and told to start your own company, what kind of people would you hire? Which of your friends, colleagues, or relatives would you hire first? Businessman Andrew Carnegie was able to assemble the greatest private-enterprise leadership team of his day. And to achieve this feat, he looked far beyond his immediate circle of friends and acquaintances.

Carnegie searched the world for the top women and men in their various fields of expertise. At one point, he found a chemist in Germany, a man who was known as the best of the best. Carnegie lured the chemist away from his current job by doubling his salary, giving him a new house, and providing the security of a five-year employment contract.

However, after only three months, Carnegie called the chemist into his office and fired him. He bought out the rest of the man's contract and paid his moving expenses back to Germany.

Why would a smart businessman like Carnegie forfeit his substantial investment and remove an elite scientist from his company? Because, as Carnegie and the chemist's new co-workers quickly discovered, the man was impossible to get along with. He constantly argued with his colleagues, hindering the company's progress and making lives miserable in the process.

Explaining his decision, Carnegie declared, "I will not have anyone work for me, especially in a leadership position, who does not have the quality of being able to get along with others."

Whether it's sports, music, drama, forensics, or any other activity, expertise will get you only so far – right now and in the future.

Don't focus only on developing your technical skills in a certain area; strive to build your "people" skills as well. Or, as another Carnegie, Dale, might put it, "Don't discount the value, the necessity, of making friends and influencing people."

The Bible, especially the New Testament, frequently stresses the importance of living and working together in peace. In fact, one of Jesus' final wishes before His death on the cross was for unity among His people. If you will be a peacemaker at home, on the job, and everywhere else, you have the Lord's promise that you will be blessed. (And so will the people around you.) The Message explains the concept beautifully:

"You're blessed when you can show people how to cooperate instead of compete or fight. That's when you discover who you really are, and your place in God's family." (Matthew 5:9)

To be sure, it's not easy being a peacemaker. Often, making peace means putting yourself in the middle of a conflict when you'd rather avoid it. But the promise of being blessed by God Himself makes it worth the risk, doesn't it?

Live in harmony with one another.

1 Peter 3:8

God has a **Plan B**

for dissing disappointment

"Hear the Lord ... and know you are loved."

— Sarah Mueller

What do you do with the inevitable disappointments that life hands you? Many people internalize them, let them creep into their hearts, where they fester and cause worry, pain, and despair.

Others are wiser, sharing disappointments with friends, relatives, or a pastor or counselor. People like these can be great sounding boards — and great resources for solutions to problems. But they aren't the best resource.

Do you make a habit of taking your disappointments to God? He should be your first option, not your last resort. Maybe you hesitate to share your disappointments with Him. He is, after all, dealing with wars, pollution, famine, crime, AIDS, and terrorism. You might think, "I feel guilty about complaining about my stupid problems in the face of all the important prayer requests God must be getting."

If you feel this way, give your Lord a chance. He might just surprise you with how much He cares about even the little things. He cared enough about a wedding going well that He turned water into wine. He cared enough about lots of stomachs rumbling that, on at least two occasions, He provided food for people who had come to listen to Him teach. He even cared enough about His disciple Peter's tax problem to give him a coin.

Think about the really good parents you know. Don't they care about their children's minor bumps and bruises and small problems – as well as the major injuries and serious life difficulties? Would they want their kids to hide their small struggles and keep them to themselves? Of course not. God is the same way. In fact, He will be disappointed if you don't come to Him with your disappointments!

Anyone who is having troubles should pray.

James 5:13 NCV

God has a **Plan B**

for being truly cool

"Never forget that only dead fish
always swim with the stream."

– Malcolm Muggeridge

Lemmings are small rodents who migrate in huge, furry masses. Sometimes, this practice leads to disaster, as one lemming unwittingly follows another as he tumbles off the edge of a cliff.

Not surprisingly then, no major sports team is dubbed "The Lemmings." After all, who would want to be named after a critter that blindly follows its peers, even to its own destruction?

Sadly, many people today become lemmings in the all-consuming quest to fit in with their peers, to be counted among the ranks of the cool. Thus, Christians face the challenge of representing their beliefs – without compromising their stand on morality and truth.

Being cool is more important and yet harder to define than ever. One thing we know about our ultimate role model: Jesus was not cool by today's standards.

He was an outcast, a lowly Hebrew carpenter weirdo who hung out with the bottom of the social food chain.

Even when Jesus was adored by some of His peers, it didn't last, because it was based on what they thought He could do for them. When Jesus rode into town on the donkey, they cheered because they believed He would liberate them politically.

Have you faced a situation in which peers – either overtly or covertly – have influenced you to rebel against the Lord or disrespect Him in some way? If so, you know the pressure. If not, be prepared. This is a scenario you will probably face someday.

The good news is that you can guard your heart against the pressure. Here's how:

1. Remember that your goal on earth is to be faithful, not cool or popular.

2. Choose close friends who challenge you in your faith and encourage you to follow ever closer to God. (Pray right now that the Lord will provide you encouraging friends – brothers and sisters in Christ – who will lift you up, not tear you down.)

3. Recognize crucial "moments of truth," and run from negative peer pressure as soon as you sniff it out.

Jesus is the ideal model to look to when issues of peer pressure and the "cool factor" present themselves. Jesus never cared for the world's idea of status. He defined the true essence of cool this way to his friends: Be a servant. Sure, "servant" might not sound like a thrilling moniker, but you might be surprised the adventures being a servant can bring. And besides, isn't "servant" a whole lot better than "lemming"?

The model that Jesus gave you to follow is not only more positive than the world's, it's consistent, unlike the ever-changing tides of what's cool in pop culture.

Do not conform any longer
to the pattern of this world,
but be transformed by the
renewing of your mind.

Romans 12:2

God has a **Plan B**

for turning setbacks
into victory

"Out of difficulties grow miracles."
– Jean de La Bruyère

Gene was a great amateur boxer. He packed knockout power in both hands and was destined to become a champion fighter once he turned professional.

But while still battling in the amateur ranks, Gene broke both of his hands. His doctor told him he would never be able to deliver a punch with the force he once possessed – and therefore he should abandon his quest to become a heavyweight champion. Gene's trainer agreed with the prognosis.

Gene Tunney didn't listen to them. He believed he could excel in a sport that focused on punching, even though he couldn't punch hard. "If I can't become a champion as a [power] puncher," he said, "I'll make it as a boxer."

So, knowing he could no longer rely on his two-fisted knockout attack, Tunney set out to perfect his boxing skills. He learned to bob and weave. He learned to throw accurate punches, rather than potent ones.

Before long, Gene earned his way to the biggest fight of his career, against the feared "Manassa Mauler" Jack Dempsey, for the world heavyweight title. Dempsey entered the fight as the favorite, based on his devastating punches. However, using the skills he would not have developed if not for his injuries, Tunney outboxed Dempsey and became world champion. And just to prove his upset victory was no fluke, Tunney beat Dempsey in their rematch.

Life's misfortunes can alter the paths we take toward success, just as they did for Gene Tunney. But that doesn't mean you still can't get where you want to go.

> **The race is not**
> **always to the swift,**
> **nor the battle to**
> **the strong.**
> **Ecclesiastes 9:11 MSG**

God has a **Plan B**

for living by the rules

"It is in giving oneself that one receives."

– St. Francis of Assisi

Of all the old-school rules, is there any one as enduring as the Golden Rule: "Do unto others as you would have them do unto you"? Simple. Straightforward. Timeless.

Unfortunately, some people believe that the Golden Rule isn't what it used to be. Bumper stickers proclaim permutations like "Do Unto Others Before They Do Unto You!" or "Do Unto Others – Then Split." Motivational speakers talk about winning through intimidation, and business leaders and professional sports coaches read books like *The Art of War* for inspiration and guidance.

Has the Golden Rule outlived its usefulness? Or, should it apply only toward being kind, loving, and compassionate to the people who show those characteristics to us – or to those who can help us achieve our personal or professional goals? Do you find yourself fearing you'll lose life's battles if you force yourself to "Do unto others …"?

In our hearts, we all know the answer to those questions. The Golden Rule isn't accompanied by an asterisk or a disclaimer. We should treat everyone the way we wish to be treated. Think about that the next time you encounter the various fund-raising groups in front of your local grocery store. Imagine that it was you trying to raise money for something. How would you feel about getting repeated "no, thank-yous" or hostile glares – or being ignored altogether?

What if you began to view every Salvation Army Santa, every church bake-sale table, every confused newbie driver on your local streets as not an annoyance but an opportunity to show the brand of kindness, generosity, and compassion that you would like to receive?

But the Golden Rule doesn't stop with those who might merely inconvenience us; it includes our enemies. And is there any tougher commandment than "Love your enemies"? Not tolerate them or simply do kind things for them. Love them. Those obnoxious, cruel, hateful people. The boss who treats you unfairly. The co-worker who pretends to be your friend, then backstabs you. The relative who is consistently rude and insulting.

The first step in loving our enemies is praying for them (not for their disgrace, downfall, or destruction, by the way). And when we pray for our enemies, we need to pray as much for our own attitudes and behaviors as for theirs. That way, even if our prayers don't change our enemies' ugly qualities, they will change us.

Often, the first thing to pray for, by the way, is simply the will and grace to want to love those we find unlovable.

In praying for these people, we may come to realize that they are no less attractive to God, no less deserving of His love, than we are. Further, as we experience what hard work it is to love unlovable people, we will value God's love for us more than ever.

And finally, as we practice "Do unto others," we might even turn an enemy into a friend – or at least someone who is neutral rather than hostile.

Whatever the case, whether the change happens in others or only in ourselves, when we obey the Golden Rule, we invariably find that it's still as good as gold.

So in everything,
do to others what you would have
them do to you, for this sums up
the Law and the Prophets.

Matthew 7:12

God has a **Plan B**

for making hope happen

> "If you do not hope, you will not find
> what is beyond your hopes."
>
> — St. Clement of Alexandria

When you were a child, did you ever wake up in the middle of the night and find your own room terrifying? Did unfamiliar shapes, shadows, and sounds cause you to freeze in fear? Were you shocked at how a once-familiar place, your own room, could be transformed into a chamber of horrors?

But what happened when morning came and the rising sun poured its light into your room? The shadows disappeared, and the once-terrifying shapes became familiar again. The troll crouching in the corner? Just a mound of dirty laundry. The huge stranger lurking in the closet? A mere coat on a hanger.

And the sounds – the clicks, groans, and rumbles – weren't nearly so terrifying in the bright light of day, were they?

That's the way God's hope is. It floods into your world, warming and illuminating everything in its path. Chasing away cold, evil, and despair.

Hope is a gift that God loves to give. He enjoys surprising us by fulfilling our hopes – and even granting us more than we could ever wish for or imagine. He let an old man named Simeon hold the Christ Child before he passed away. He granted another old fellow, Abraham, a son when he and his wife were well beyond child-bearing years. He turned Joseph from a slave to a mighty ruler.

Who knows how God might fulfill and surpass your hopes? It might surprise you, but it will happen. So never, never give up hope. You can count on this: Hope didn't happen only to people in Bible times. Hope happens here; hope happens now.

God will help you overflow with hope in him
through the Holy Spirit's power within you.

Romans 15:13 TLB

God has a **Plan B**

for avoiding bitterness

"Love liberates everything."
— Maya Angelou

Maybe that "pet grudge" was cute when you first got it. But it won't be for long. If you keep feeding it, encouraging it, it will grow big, demanding, and ugly. It will whine and whimper and scratch at your door and keep you up at night. And it will leave unsightly stains on your soul. Bigger and bigger stains. That's because little grudges can grow up to be huge vendettas. So, it's time to set that grudge free. The Bible says that a servant of the Lord "must not quarrel; instead, he must be kind to everyone ... not resentful." (2 Timothy 2:24)

Open your heart's door and shoo the grudge away. Then, forgive the person who gave it to you in the first place. You will feel better; that's a promise. Your heart will feel lighter. And if that grudge ever finds its way back to you and scratches at your door, pretend you are not home.

Remember, if you hold grudges, you won't be able to hold much else.

There's another problem with holding on to a grudge, harboring bitterness and unforgiveness in your heart.

A young boy named T.R. became so enthralled with skunks that he decided to get a couple as pets – by catching them in the wild. In his tiny second-grade brain, he reasoned that if he found young skunks ("skunk puppies," he called them) and spoke to them in soothing tones and treated them gently, they wouldn't spray him. And, he reasoned, even if they did, young skunks wouldn't be able to produce the kind of eye-stinging stench as the full-grown versions.

T.R. was wrong on all counts. Yes, the two skunks were cuddly and non-aggressive when he first scooped them up into his arms and carried them to their new home: the family milk box. However, the first time he opened the milk box lid to check on his new pets, he received a double-shot of skunk spray, right in the face.

He was not allowed in the house for several hours – hours which included being sprayed down with the garden hose at regular intervals. And even then, it took many rounds in the bathtub, with alternating regimens of tomato juice and Mr. Bubble, before anyone in the family, including the family dog, would go near him. (And that dog, it should be noted, regularly rolled in garbage, drank out of the toilet, and dragged home a variety of body parts from dead animals.)

But, and here's the point of this true-life adventure, the skunk stench didn't just repel T.R.'s family; it made the boy himself wish he could escape from his own skin, his own senses. Because he could perceive only one thing: skunk. Even his mom's famous cherry pie, which she baked to comfort her son in his hour of need, might as well have been skunk pie – because that's all he could smell or taste.

Bitterness is like concentrated Eau de Skunk. It pollutes how we perceive the rest of the world. Pizza doesn't smell and taste as savory when your head is filled with bitterness. The world looks dingy and dark when viewed through lenses smudged and smeared with unforgiveness.

You might have really been hurt. Betrayed. Backstabbed. Lied about. Harassed. Bullied. It stinks; there's no getting around it. But you have to let the bitterness go. You need to forgive.

What if the person who hurt you didn't ask for forgiveness? What if the person doesn't seem sorry?

Consider Jesus' example. Remember what He said when He was bleeding and fighting for breath while dying on the cross? "Father, forgive them, for they know not what they do." Were his tormentors sorry? No. In fact, many of them were mocking Him in His time of agony. He forgave them anyway.

How about a different example? Remember the paraplegic man, lowered by friends – through a roof – right in front of Jesus? What is the first thing Jesus said to him? "Your sins are forgiven." That wasn't why the guys brought their friend to Jesus. And, to be sure, this poor guy was much more concerned with being able to do the Running Man (or even the Walking Man) than having his sins forgiven. But Jesus recognized his deepest need and took care of that one first.

In a similar vein, you may have people in your life who don't want – or think they need – forgiveness. But by showing forgiveness and mercy to them, you just might rock their world. Yours, too.

Therefore, rid yourselves of all malice.

1 Peter 2:1

God has a **Plan B**

for building grace-full
relationships

"Humanity is never so beautiful as when
praying forgiveness or else forgiving another."
– Jean Paul Richter

Human relationships will never be perfect until we all get to heaven. Until that day, our interactions with family and friends will be sources of great joy, but also extreme frustration and even deep pain.

God created relationships and gave us the perfect model of how they should look. We were meant to love each other, to serve each other, and to put others' needs ahead of our own.

The world's version of relationship is, quite often, selfish. Think about how many times you've been asked, "What do you look for in a friend?" "What's your idea of the perfect date?"

Conversely, have you ever been asked, "What do you hope you can bring to your friendships?" "What kind of romantic partner do you aspire to be?" Did those last two questions seem odd? Thank the 21st Century's mantra: All Me, All the Time. Have you ever heard of anyone ending a romance or a friendship by (honestly) saying, "I don't think I was bringing enough to our relationship. I wasn't doing enough for you"? Nope, it's all about "What's in it for me?" "What have you done for me lately?" "Are you meeting my needs?"

Is it any wonder that we tend to approach relationships with suspicious eyes, half-closed hearts, or worse – a "get them before they get you" attitude?

God did not intend for us to live in this bizarre relationship economy, in which we try to gain as much as we can from others while giving as little as we can get away with.

A friendship, romance, or family relationship built on that economic model is going to bankrupt people before long. Relationships work best under God's model. If we, with an open heart, love each other, serve each other, and put our own agenda last on the list, we reap big, hefty bushels of love and joy in return. Does this sound like a paradox? It is. Welcome to the Christian faith, an entire way of life built on paradox. A small seed becomes a huge tree. Those who are willing to wait at the end of the line end up getting upgraded to the front. Give stuff away like there's no tomorrow, and you get it back with interest. Clutch onto stuff with a kung-fu grip, and it'll wither and die and slip right out of your hands. Serve people humbly, and you'll become a leader.

What does this have to do with your relationship with your co-workers, siblings, friends, or romantic person of interest? Simple: If you are keeping score with any of the above people, you are playing the wrong game.

It's best to put away the scorecards when it comes to your relationships. Start asking yourself questions like, "What can I bring to the table in my relationships?" "What needs do those around me have – and how can I help meet them?" "What can I do that will delight the people in my life? Surprise them? Honor them? Show them God's love?"

This approach, the one Jesus modeled so well, will set you free – turn you loose to be the kind of friend, son, daughter, sibling, boyfriend, girlfriend, spouse, whatever that people will thank God for. Wouldn't you like to play the relationship game this way, not the world's way? If so, it's your turn to serve.

Serve one another in love.

Galatians 5:13

God has a **Plan B**

for silencing your critics

> **"God loves to hear his children laugh.**
> **What healthy father doesn't?"**
>
> – Mark Lowry

The famous British leader Winston Churchill had just finished a rousing speech. Upon his final words, the crowd who had gathered to hear him erupted with a thunderous ovation. However, when the clapping and cheering ceased, one man, unimpressed by Sir Winston's rhetoric, blew him "the raspberry."

The rest of the audience froze in suspense, awaiting the powerful statesman's response to the rude critic. Would he scream at the man, publicly humiliate him? Would he have him thrown out of the audience? Churchill looked at his tormentor and then spoke.

"I know," he said good-naturedly. "I agree with you. But what are we among so many?"

Churchill's humble and humorous reply was a hit with the throng, and the tense situation was quickly diffused.

Like Sir Winston, you might occasionally face insults or criticism from a jealous or mean-spirited nemesis. In such cases, it's tempting to become angry and lose your composure. And in today's power-is-everything world, conventional wisdom tells people to be defiant in the face of criticism, to fight fire with fire. Unfortunately, this approach usually leads to someone getting burned.

Don't forget the power of humility and humor to relax a tense situation. The Bible promises that a soft answer turns away wrath. Certainly, there will be times when you must forcefully defend yourself or a friend. Be watchful, however, for those times when a clever, self-deprecating comeback can disarm even the most hostile of foes, the harshest of critics.

Remember: Because you have God's love, you are rich – rich enough to be able to afford some jokes at your own expense.

Sensible people keep their eyes glued on wisdom.

Proverbs 17:24 NLT

God has a **Plan B**

for reaching goals

"I know God will not give me anything I can't handle.
I just wish He didn't trust me so much."

– Mother Teresa

Watch a televised marathon, and you'll see an interesting phenomenon. As the starter's gun fires, a few novice runners will sprint to the front of the pack. These attention-grabbers want a few moments on camera – and they want to be able to boast to friends, "I led the marathon! I was in first place! Did you see me?"

However, while these people might get the attention they crave at the start of the race, you probably won't see them crossing the finish line 26+ miles later – unless they are walking. That's because they know how to get a fast start, but they can't finish strong. Finishing a marathon requires patience, perspective, endurance, strength, and just plain grit. It's a lot like life itself.

Almost anyone can approach life's endeavors with an initially high level of energy and enthusiasm. Unfortunately, many of these endeavors can drain one's energy and flatten one's enthusiasm. The truly successful people are those who can maintain their commitment to a goal over the long haul.

You can bring a champion marathoner's approach to your life's goals – ensuring that you will start fresh and finish strong – by following the three Ps.

The first key is preparation. Remember those glory-hound runners from the first paragraph? They couldn't finish well the race they started so briskly because they weren't prepared for the long challenge before them. They didn't train well or adapt a smart diet to prepare their bodies. They didn't read books or articles on marathoning or formulate a race plan to ensure they were mentally and tactically ready.

Preparation can help you succeed at any endeavor. If, for example, you want to lose a few pounds, prepare yourself by reading what qualified people have to say about the subject. Talk with family members or friends who have been successful at shedding weight and keeping it off. Seek their advice. Enlist their support.

The second key is perspective. (Hey, have you gotten the idea that this concept is really important?) A marathoner realizes that he has a long race before him, so he doesn't get caught up in the early excitement and expend too much energy at the beginning. He paces himself. He strives for a "negative split" – meaning he sets out to run the second half of the race faster than the first.

That's because of a long-time racing axiom that warns: For every minute you run too fast in the first half of the race, you will lose twice that amount in the second half. You can adapt the same principle of balance and perspective. If you're a student, for example, don't load up on too many hard classes in one quarter or semester. Try to build a schedule that's balanced. You can apply this principle on a smaller level, too. When you're preparing for a test, don't leave all the mental "heavy lifting" for the night before.

Perspective doesn't just help you handle the work at hand; it also helps you develop a proper attitude toward that work. When a marathoner hits the mid-point of his race, for example, he doesn't think, "Oh, no, I still have a long way to go!" Instead, he tells himself, "All right! I've already come a long way. From this point, I don't even have to run a marathon anymore – it's just a half marathon!"

The final "P" is perseverance. Almost any goal requires perseverance. That's because almost any goal will present obstacles and disappointments. Even with all the preparation and perspective in the world, you may reach a point of mental and physical fatigue as you strive to finish what you've started.

Times like these require good old-fashioned staying power. Willpower. Determination. You'll face moments when you must remind yourself of what your goal is, how much it means to you, and how you will feel if you don't achieve it. Then, you take one more stride, eat one more carrot stick (instead of a Twinkie), read one more chapter, take one more test. Perseverance isn't always pretty, but it works. Just ask Thomas Edison, who failed hundreds and hundreds of times before coming up with a properly functioning light bulb.

You might not have the lung capacity of an elite marathon runner or the scientific acumen of an Edison, but you can match their determination. And when you finish what you've begun, you can share in their triumph as well.

Let us run with perseverance
the race marked out for us.
Let us fix our eyes on Jesus,
the author and perfecter of our faith.

Hebrews 12:1-2

God has a **Plan B**

for strengthening the weak

"God loves you simply because he has chosen to do so.
He loves you when you don't feel lovely.
He loves you when no one else loves you."

– Max Lucado

If you've taken an astronomy class in your academic career,
you probably have some idea about the vastness of space.
But did you know ...

- Astronomers have discovered galaxies that are billions and billions
  of light years away from ours. When you gaze up at the stars at
  night, do you realize that the light you are seeing from them is

actually millions of years old? Some stars are so old, in fact, that by the time their light reaches us, they have already died or collapsed.

- We tend to think of our sun as a major entity, but it's actually rather mediocre, as stars go. For example, the star Eta Carinae outshines the sun the same way a giant spotlight outshines a tiny spark.

- The universe is populated with neutron stars so dense that one teaspoon of its mass weighs thousands of pounds.

Who wouldn't marvel at the power of a God who created a universe so vast and spectacular? But, have you stopped to realize that all of that power is available to you? The Bible says that even the power God used to raise Jesus from the dead can be tapped into by His followers.

So don't let life's challenges overwhelm you. You truly have a Friend in high places. Face today's problems with today's God-given strength and wisdom. Don't spend time or energy worrying about future troubles. Some of them won't even come about. And with the others, God will provide for you when the time is right. Remember that God's guidance is a "light unto our feet," not a high-intensity spotlight that penetrates miles into the future.

The God who established the universe wants to establish your life's path, one day at a time, one step at a time.

I can do all things through Christ who strengthens me.

Philippians 4:13 NKJV

God has a **Plan B**

for accepting grief and loss as
part of life

"I have been driven many times to my knees
by the overwhelming conviction
that I had nowhere else to go."
– Abraham Lincoln

We live in a fallen world, and as a result, we all experience pain. The hurt of a loved one lost will affect every one of us at some point. That's sobering news, but here's some good news to balance it: The pain, the questions, the helpless feelings – God is Lord over all of it.

He never said our journey would be without heartaches, without loss. From our earthly perspective, the death of a loved one is devastating in its apparent finality. Yet, from God's eternal, all-knowing perspective, it's just a temporary separation.

This is not to say that He doesn't hurt with us, and for us. Remember the famous "shortest verse in the Bible"? John 11:35 says "Jesus wept." Why did He cry?

In John's account, Jesus' good friend Lazarus died, and Jesus arrived at the burial site after getting the news. Jesus knew that in a few seconds, He was going to tell Lazarus to rise up and come out of his tomb. Yet He still cried. He was deeply moved.

Why? Did the fully human aspect of Jesus simply miss His friend? Or were His tears more for Lazarus' friends and family – tears of empathy? Maybe it was a combination of both.

God knows when you are hurting, and He feels the hurt right along with you. That is something we can take comfort in. When we hurt, finding someone who understands allows us to be open with our emotions. We don't have to worry about being looked at as if we are crazy. We can be honest and authentic before God.

Of course, God is more than empathetic and understanding. He is loving, wise, all-powerful, and eternal. This means that, someday, we will see His whole plan and how He orchestrated it all through history. We'll see that He was beside us, loving us and working through us, even in our times of heartbreak.

For now, we can rest in the understanding that God's plan is good; He wants to give us a future filled with hope. And He will make good on His promise to work all things for our good if we love and serve Him. This doesn't mean that everything that happens in our lives will be good. It isn't good for you when a relative or close friend dies. But God will be your comfort and your hope in those times. And He will bring good from those tragedies. Family bonds can be strengthened. Friendships can be rekindled. Priorities can be put in their proper order.

This world can hurt sometimes. But it's possible, even through our tears, to try to look ahead with hope. This world is not our home. Heaven is a real place, and we will see it – and all its citizens – soon enough. Then we will grieve no more.

Yes, grief is a weight we might have to carry for a long time. But, thank God, we don't have to carry it alone.

Rest in the knowledge that you cannot go anywhere – even the depths of despair – where God cannot reach.

God blesses those who mourn,

for they will be comforted.

Matthew 5:4 NLT

God has a **Plan B**

for providing small blessings

"God speaks to each of us in the beauty of every flower,
in the grace of every tree, in the shimmer of every star."

– Carolyn Hoppe

On a cool spring afternoon, an expert wood carver sat on his front
porch, sipping lemonade and enjoying the view. Around him on the
porch sat his various creations. A friend of the carver's stopped by for
a quick visit and was surprised to see the artisan relaxing. "It's only
1:30 in the afternoon," the friend observed, "a little early in the day
for a break, isn't it?"

The artisan swallowed a mouthful of lemonade and yawned. "This isn't
a break," he answered. "I'm done for the day."

The friend, a young marketing executive, was puzzled. "What do you mean? It's too early in the day for you to stop carving. You need to produce more. If you carve more figures, you can make more money. You could even hire an assistant to help you with the business end of things. You could buy new tools. You could buy a shop, so you wouldn't have to carve here at your house."

"Why would I want to do all of that?" the carver asked.

"So you can make more money! Are you dense?" his friend sputtered.

"And what would I do with all that extra money?"

"Why, enjoy life, of course!"

The carver sipped his lemonade again, then leaned back in his chair and closed his eyes. Before he drifted off into an afternoon nap, he mumbled contentedly, "Enjoy life? What do you think I'm doing right now?"

The lesson here? God provides an abundance of blessings every day. Make sure you don't get too busy to enjoy them.

Make sure that your character is free from the love of money, being content with what you have.

Hebrews 13:5 NASB

God has a **Plan B**

for honoring humanity's inherent value

"Beauty comes in all ages, colors, shapes, and forms.
God never makes junk."

– Kathy Ireland

A medical school professor once posed this bio-ethics question to a group of students: "Here's a family history. The father has syphilis. The mother has TB. They already have four children. The first is blind. The second has died. The third is deaf. The fourth has TB. Now the mother is pregnant again. The parents come to you for advice. They are willing to abort their child if you decide they should. What do you say?"

After the students shared various opinions, the prof placed them into groups to make final decisions. After deliberating, every group reported that it would recommend an abortion to the parents.

"Congratulations," the professor told his class. "You just took the life of Beethoven!"

The lesson here? A person's inherent value and potential don't depend on family background or social status or even likelihood of success in life. God creates each person with worth and skill and promise. The way you treat those around you shouldn't be tainted by a prejudice based on race, economic status, physical appearance, or handicap. This advice might seem like a no-brainer, but many people are shocked when they honestly evaluate the way they perceive and treat others.

Like Beethoven, every person has potential to add music to the great symphony called life. That includes the people you encounter in life. And that includes you, too.

You – and everyone around you – have way more potential than you have history or heritage.

Accept one another, then, just as Christ accepted you, in order to bring praise to God.

Romans 15:7

God has a **Plan B**

for unity

"Happiness is only in loving."

– Leo Tolstoy

Jesus' last formal prayer before He died on the cross was for unity within the body of Christ. As He awaited the most terrible ordeal a human has ever faced, Jesus took the time to pray that "those who will believe in me ... may become one. May they be brought to complete unity." (John 17:20-23)

Sadly, today that body has been wounded and disjointed – not so much from outside assaults, but by quarrels from within. Churches split and splinter with regularity. And many authors and artists are attacked for their alleged "incorrect" beliefs and motives. All the while, the world that Christians are called to witness to is watching.

Think about your life. Are there religious cliques at your job – even within your church? Have you found yourself being criticized for the kind of music you listen to (e.g., "There's no way rock music can be Christian!"), the denomination you belong to, or the TV shows you watch?

Imagine the impact Christians could have on the world if we quit fighting among ourselves. Want to help bring about unity and make a difference in the lives of those around you? Here are a few suggestions:

- Be humble, and encourage humility in others. Humility is a wellspring of Christian unity. As Philippians 2 teaches, "In humility consider others better than yourself."

- Don't label people. Labels demean. They stifle opportunities for fellowship, they blind us to the good in others, and they emphasize differences rather than common ground.

- Avoid gossip. Gossip has destroyed friendships, fueled feuds, and even splintered entire churches. Gossip is tempting. To help resist the temptation, keep in mind that the Bible says that the Lord hates a person who stirs up dissension among fellow believers.

For Christians to effectively connect with a lost world, we must stop fighting among ourselves. You can't pull a truck out of a ditch with one tiny thread – or even hundreds of individual threads. However, if you weave the threads together, they can become a strong rope that is strong enough for the task at hand.

In the same manner, it's time for Christians to lay aside their differences, join forces, and pull together.

Every kingdom divided against itself
is brought to desolation, and every city or house
divided against itself will not stand.

Matthew 12:25 NKJV

God has a **Plan B**

for helping you
overcome adversity

"Success is going from failure to failure
without losing your enthusiasm."

– Abraham Lincoln

A group of frogs was hopping through the woods. Suddenly, two of them plunged into a deep pit, which had been covered by loose grass and weeds. As the other frogs circled the pit, they quickly concluded that their amphibious friends were doomed. Frantically, the two misfortunate frogs began leaping with all their strength.

"Give it up," their cohorts scolded them. "You are as good as dead."

But still the two frogs kept jumping.

After a half-hour, one of the trapped frogs became discouraged, curled up in a dark corner of the pit, and waited to die. But the other frog kept leaping, even though his companions above the pit continued to jeer.

Finally, with one mighty lunge, the frog propelled himself to the top of the pit, barely grasping its rim, then pulled his way to safety. "Wow! You sure have hops!" one of the surprised frogs shouted. "I guess it was a good thing you ignored our taunts."

The now-safe frog looked at his companions, a puzzled expression on his green face. Then, through a series of frog sign-language gestures, the creature explained to the others that he was deaf and couldn't hear anything. In fact, the frog signed, when he saw their frantic gestures and flapping frog jaws, he assumed they were encouraging him!

The lesson here: You can accomplish amazing feats when you turn a deaf ear – or two – to the discouraging words of negative-thinking naysayers.

For it is God's will that by doing good you should silence the ignorant talk of foolish men.

1 Peter 2:15

God has a **Plan B**

for rewarding your diligence

"Where our work is, there let our joy be."

– Tertullian

Long ago, there were two jars. Each was carried by a king's water bearer on opposite ends of a long pole. One jar was perfectly made, with no cracks or chips. The other was unglazed earthenware with a long, jagged crack at its base.

Daily, the water bearer would walk to a river and fill both containers, then carry them to the king's palace. Once inside, the first jar offered its full contents into the king's cistern. The other had less to offer, since most of its contents had leaked through the crack during the journey.

One day, the despondent cracked jar pleaded with the water bearer, "Please, sir, replace me. I am a failure. I spill so much that my offering cannot compare to what the perfect jar brings. I'm ashamed!"

The water bearer smiled in response. "Take a look at the hill we climb each day," he said. The jar obeyed. All along the path bloomed beautiful wildflowers. "I've been planting seeds as I walk up this hill," noted the water bearer. "And those flowers you see have grown from your water, little jar. Flowers that please the king and all his people."

Like the jar in this tale, if you do your job diligently, you will be able to survey the landscape of your life and see the flowers of faithfulness that you have grown. Not because you are perfect, but because you were faithful to your task.

Never tire of doing what is right.

2 Thessalonians 3:13

God has a **Plan B**

for transforming errors
into successes

"The two most powerful warriors are patience and time."
— Leo Tolstoy

"I speak without exaggeration," Thomas Edison once said, "when I say that I have constructed three thousand different theories in connection with electric light, each one of them reasonable and apparently likely to be true. Yet in two cases only did my experiments prove the truth of my theory."

Think about the quote above, then do the math: Thomas Edison, a renowned scientific genius, developed 2,998 failed theories in order to produce two successful experiments. In fact, the entire story of the light bulb is a tedious tale of repeated trial and failure. Yet, through it all, Edison was watching attentively and learning from each mistake, each false start.

Another lesson can be learned from Edison's adventures with electricity: As his various attempts to carbonize a cotton thread and use it as a light bulb filament failed, Edison realized that he had to combine extraordinary determination with his extraordinary care and patience. Matching the right thread thickness with the right carbonization technique was painstaking work, and Edison knew that the more intent he became about his task, the more patience and precision he needed to avoid ruining or misreading the results of his earnest efforts.

So, follow Edison's lead. When failures mount up, step back. Re-examine what you are doing. Ask God for His precious gift of patience. And remember, patience is more of a decision than an emotion. And it's a foundational part of good character.

As you develop and test your own bright ideas, remember and emulate the patience exemplified by people like Thomas Edison. If you are patient and prayerful about your problems, solutions will come to light.

Patience is better than pride.

Ecclesiastes 7:8

God has a **Plan B**

for lightening your load

"To be a Christian without prayer is no more possible
than to be alive without breathing."

– Martin Luther

Do you ever feel you're on information overload? Cell phone buzzing
or jangling all the time? E-mails building up faster than you can
answer them? Answering machine blinking incessantly? Pop-up ads
invading your Web searches? The boss asking when that project will
be done?

Believe it or not, Jesus knows how you feel. True, the only 'Net that
He dealt with was the kind used to catch fish. But He did know the
stress of having so many people crowd around Him that sometimes
He and the disciples didn't even get a chance to eat. On at least

one occasion, He had to preach from a boat, just to keep from being suffocated by an eager audience. (And speaking of fishing, on at least one other occasion, Jesus was so exhausted by all the demands placed on Him that He fell asleep in the bottom of a hard, uncomfortable fishing boat – in the middle of a violent sea storm.)

Indeed, your Lord understands the fatigue of information/obligation overload. And He provides a great example of how to deal with it. In the book of Mark, the writer tells us: "Early the next morning, while it was still dark, Jesus woke and left the house. He went to a lonely place, where he prayed." (Mark 1:35 NCV)

Now, you might not be crazy about the "early morning" thing, but if even God's Son Himself needed some private, quiet time, that should speak volumes to you.

Your Lord understands the pressure you feel, the barrage of information that bombards you every day. So find a quiet place, a quiet time, through which you can bring your stresses to Him. Vent. Cry if you need to. Ask for help.

Just remember that whenever you're on overload, there is someone who can share that load with you. And one of the best ways to hear His voice is to put yourself in a place where that voice is the only one you can hear.

> **Don't worry about anything;**
> **instead, pray about everything.**
> **Tell God what you need,**
> **and thank him for all he has done.**
> Philippians 4:6 NLT

God has a **Plan B**

for blessing you big-time!

"God loves each one of us
as if there were only one of us."
– St. Augustine

Magic moments. You've had them. Chugging a bubbling soda after a hot day of outdoor work. Standing and cheering at the end of an inspiring song at a concert. Holding a little child's hand on a walk to the park or ice cream shop. Seeing that familiar smile burst across your best friend's face when you unexpectedly bump into each other at the mall. Having a relative mention your name when thanking God for His blessings.

Every good and perfect moment like this is a gift to you from God. Every one – even the ones that seem like happenstance or coincidence. He sends these gifts to remind us all that He is still in control, and that His supply of love and kindness will never run dry. And because of this, life is always worth living.

These gifts also remind us to keep our eyes, minds, and hearts open for the blessings, large and small, that await us in the future. Instead of dreading all that might go wrong tomorrow, next month, or next year, we should spend our energy being watchful for those magic moments, the ones that fill our mouths with laughter and make us want to shout with joy.

So the next time God drops one of these blessings on your tongue, take time to savor it, enjoy it. A seemingly momentary blessing can leave a sweet aftertaste that can last forever – so let it.

God will load your world with gifts, large and small. Take the time to open them all!

He will yet fill your mouth with laughter
and your lips with shouts of joy.

Job 8:21

God has a **Plan B**

for punching out procrastination

"Make each day your masterpiece."

– Coach John Wooden

Do any of these statements sound familiar to you?

"Someday I'll take my kids to the movies."

"Someday I'll volunteer to do some community service."

"Someday I'll start attending church regularly again."

"Someday I'll call or E-mail my old friend – as soon as things get less crazy."

Good intentions are fine, but there is a problem with "someday" statements. Sometimes, someday never comes. Opportunities vanish. Kids grow up and move out. Lukewarm friendships go stone-cold.

Heaven knows that life can be busy. But it's your life, and it's up to you how you will spend it. Don't let opportunities to reach out and touch the lives of others slip through your fingers.

Make an effort. Set priorities. Give yourself some time limits if you must. Send that letter or E-mail. Make that phone call. Buy that gift. Put your name on that volunteer list. Get committed. Do something kind for that adorable little kid while he or she is still little.

Don't look at time as a prison. Think of it as a gift from God. Then, as you sort through your life's priorities, think of how God would want you to use His gift of time. Would He want you to seize those opportunities to do good or to neglect them?

All hard work brings a profit,
but mere talk leads only to poverty.

Proverbs 14:23

God has a **Plan B**

for leading you through difficult times

"God's promises are like the stars;
the darker the night, the brighter they shine."

— David Nicholas

One night, a group of people staying in a remote tropical resort had to be evacuated from their building. All of the power was shut off due to a gas leak, and guests were instructed to abandon the resort quickly.

As the guests clustered outside, an assistant manager ordered, "It's pitch black out tonight, so everyone stay together and follow me. We must go right now; it would be too dangerous and time-consuming to go back into the building and try to find a flashlight."

"But we can't see anything," one guest protested. "Our eyes haven't adjusted to the dark yet – they're useless."

"It's OK," the assistant manager replied. "Let me be your eyes. I have been outside on my break, so my eyes are adjusted. Besides, I know this area well. I can lead you to safety. Just stay close to me; stay close to the sound of my voice."

As the group began to make its way through the tropical island's tall weeds and thick underbrush, a few members began to complain. "I can't see a thing, and there are wild animals out here," one said. "What if I get bitten by a poisonous spider or fall in a hole?" another grumbled. "I can't even see my hand in front of my face."

"That's OK," their guide assured. "I can see everything."

The guests obeyed, although many of them were afraid and confused for the entire journey. Eventually, everyone made it to another resort, where they were able to stay until their safe return could be arranged.

The guide in this story didn't get rid of all the thick jungle foliage for those he led. Nor did he rid the area of wild animals and poisonous spiders and snakes. But he still led them safely.

Jesus is like the guide in this story. He doesn't give us the gift of a danger-free, obstacle-free life. Instead, He gives us the gift of Himself. He promises to serve as our guide on every step of life's journey. The terrain might be treacherous, but He can lead us over it.

The Lord will guide you always; he will satisfy your needs.

Isaiah 58:11

God has a **Plan B**

for facing failure

"Obstacles cannot crush me.
Every obstacle yields to stern resolve."

– Leonardo da Vinci

If you have recently bitten into a bitter mouthful of disappointment, don't let it ruin your appetite for life. You are in good company. Consider the following examples:

- NBA superstar Michael Jordan was once cut from his high school basketball team.

- After his first audition, screen legend Fred Astaire received the following assessment from an MGM executive: "Can't act. Slightly bald. Can dance a little."

- Best-selling author Max Lucado had his first book rejected by 14 publishers before finding one that was willing to give him a chance.

- A so-called football expert once said of two-time Super Bowl-winning coach Vince Lombardi, "He possesses minimal football knowledge. Lacks motivation."

- Walt Disney was fired from a newspaper because he lacked ideas. Later, he went bankrupt several times before he built Disneyland.

- Upon his election as U.S. President, Abraham Lincoln was called "a baboon" by a newspaper in Illinois, his home state. The paper went on to say that the American people "would be better off if he were assassinated."

- A young Burt Reynolds was once told he couldn't act. At the same audition, his pal Clint Eastwood was told he would never make it in the movies because his Adam's apple was too big.

But none of these people let discouraging words etch themselves in their hearts. They knew that one can learn a truckload from rejection and disappointment. For example, you might discover a weakness that you need to bolster to reach your maximum potential. You might learn that people's judgments about you are highly subjective and that one key to success is simply finding someone who understands you and believes in you. All opinions about you are not created equal – or accurate.

Further, failure can actually enrich you as a person, build your character, and sharpen your perspective. Andre Agassi, after winning easily in the first round of a U.S. Open tennis tourney, was asked if he felt bad for destroying his opponent. "No," he said, "you don't cheat anybody out of their experience, whatever it is. I promise you, it's all part of what makes you who you are down the road. And if a match is getting blown out one way or the other, you've got to learn from it, and you've got to understand it for what it is. I've been on the other [losing] side. I wouldn't want to cheat anybody of that experience."

So, learn from failure, from rejection. Let them fuel your determination. And hang on to those negative letters, reports, and evaluations. You might want to frame them someday.

Let us not become weary in doing good,
for at the proper time we will reap
a harvest if we do not give up.

Galatians 6:9

God has a **Plan B**

for transforming us with love

"Love makes you bold. Love makes you beautiful."

– Terrence Howard

Jesus' love changed a lot of people. Paul turned from a heartless persecutor of Christians to a heart-on-his-sleeve encourager and self-sacrificing missionary. Zaccheus was transformed from a shrewd, greedy taker of money to a repentant, openhearted giver.

One of the most dramatic transformations occurs early in the Gospel of John. Jesus, who is Jewish, meets a woman who is Samaritan, a people hated by Jews. Further, she has gone through five husbands and is currently living with a man she is not married to. That's scandalous, even by today's standards.

But Jesus talks with her, which amazes her. (In fact, it shocks even His disciples.) The Lord doesn't judge her. Instead, He offers her (again, a sworn enemy of the Jewish people) the "fresh, living water" of salvation.

Finally, Jesus inspires her (some theologians say He actually assigned her) to go into her village and tell everyone about Him.

It's significant that the villagers responded to her words and went to see the Messiah for themselves. Why did they trust the words of a woman of dubious reputation – a woman who admitted to conversing with "the enemy"? They must have been able to sense that her loving encounter with Jesus had changed her forever.

Jesus' love can do the same for you – no matter what you have done. His love can soothe the pain and shame of your past and give you energy, hope, and purpose for your future. Jesus has been using love to transform lives for thousands of years; He's quite good at it. Let Him show you, personally.

> I'll call nobodies and make them somebodies;
> I'll call the unloved and make them beloved.
>
> Romans 9:25 MSG

God has a **Plan B**

more words from The Word

The following pages contain some favorite Bible verses,
as an additional resource to help assure you
of God's love and faithfulness – and to help you discover
and better understand God's plans for your life.

God's character

God is faithful, by whom ye were called
unto the fellowship of his Son Jesus Christ our Lord.

1 Corinthians 1:9 KJV

Do not fear, for I am with you; do not be dismayed,
for I am your God. I will strengthen you ... with
my righteous right hand.

Isaiah 41:10

The Lord saw how great man's wickedness on the earth
had become ... his heart was only evil all the time.
The Lord was grieved that he had made man on the earth,
and his heart was filled with pain.

Genesis 6:5-6

Blessed be the Lord your God,
who delighted in you.

1 Kings 10:9 NKJV

Never will I leave you; never will I forsake you.

Hebrews 13:5

The Lord is watching his children,
listening to their prayers.

1 Peter 3:12 TLB

God's love and care
for His people

My grace is sufficient for thee:
for my strength is made perfect in weakness.

2 Corinthians 12:9 KJV

The Lord will guide you always;
He will satisfy your needs.

Isaiah 58:11

I have come that they may have life,
and that they may have it more abundantly.

John 10:10 NKJV

My sheep recognize my voice, and I know them,
and they follow me. I give them eternal life
and they shall never perish.
No one shall snatch them away from me.

John 10:27-28 TLB

You created my inmost being; you knit me together
in my mother's womb. I praise you
because I am fearfully and wonderfully made.

Psalm 139:13-14

God's faithfulness

There shall not any man be able to stand before thee
all the days of thy life: as I was with Moses,
so I will be with thee: I will not fail thee,
nor forsake thee.

Joshua 1:5 KJV

Those who hope in the Lord will renew their strength.
They will soar on wings like eagles; they will run
and not grow weary, they will walk and not be faint.

Isaiah 40:31

Your word is a lamp to my feet and a light for my path.

Psalm 119:105

I will forgive their wickedness
and will remember their sins no more.

Hebrews 8:12

perspective

And we know that in all things God works for the good
of those who love him, who have been called
according to his purpose.

Romans 8:28

A cheerful heart is good medicine.

Proverbs 17:22

Don't worry about anything; instead, pray about
everything; tell God your needs and don't forget
to thank him for his answers. If you do this
you will experience God's peace, which is far more
wonderful than the human mind can understand.
His peace will keep your thoughts and your hearts
quiet and at rest as you trust in Christ Jesus.

Philippians 4:6-7 TLB

Cast your cares on the Lord and he will sustain you.

Psalm 55:22

Where your treasure is, there your heart will be also.

Matthew 6:21

Be joyful in hope, patient in affliction,
faithful in prayer.

Romans 12:12

humanity's responsibility to God

Love the Lord your God with all your heart
and with all your soul and with all your strength.

Deuteronomy 6:5

Remember your Creator in the days of your youth.

Ecclesiastes 12:1

What does the Lord require of you? To act justly and to love
mercy and to walk humbly with your God.

Micah 6:8

Do not neglect your gift.

1 Timothy 4:14

If you love me, you will obey what I command.

John 14:15

Whatever you do, work at it with all your heart,
as working for the Lord, not for men.

Colossians 3:23

true success

What good will it be for a man if he gains
the whole world, yet forfeits his soul?

Matthew 16:26

The memory of the righteous will be a blessing,
but the name of the wicked will rot.

Proverbs 10:7

Be on your guard against all kinds of greed;
a man's life does not consist in the abundance
of his possessions.

Luke 12:15

Whoever wishes to become great among you
shall be your servant.

Matthew 20:26 NASB

A good name is to be chosen rather than great riches,
loving favor rather than silver and gold.

Proverbs 22:1 NKJV

love

Do everything in love.

1 Corinthians 16:14

A new command I give you: Love one another.
As I have loved you, so you must love one another.

John 13:34

Above all, love each other deeply,
because love covers over a multitude of sins.

1 Peter 4:8

Dear friends, let us love one another,
for love comes from God.

1 John 4:7

Whoever does not love does not know God,
because God is love.

1 John 4:8

If we love one another, God lives in us
and his love is made complete in us.

1 John 4:12

living in harmony with others

Be patient with each other, making allowance
for each other's faults because of your love.

Ephesians 4:2 TLB

Accept one another, then, just as Christ accepted you,
in order to bring praise to God.

Romans 15:7

Honor one another above yourselves.

Romans 12:10

Be compassionate and humble.

1 Peter 3:8

Bear with each other and forgive whatever grievances you
may have against one another.
Forgive as the Lord forgave you.

Colossians 3:13

If you spend yourselves in behalf of the hungry
and satisfy the needs of the oppressed, then your light will
rise in the darkness, and your night
will become like the noonday.

Isaiah 58:10

If you are angry, don't sin by nursing your grudge.

Ephesians 4:26 TLB

Live in peace with each other.

1 Thessalonians 5:13

Blessed are the merciful, for they will be shown mercy.

Matthew 5:7

Be kind to one another, tenderhearted,
forgiving one another, as God in Christ forgave you.

Ephesians 4:32 RSV

inner peace

Do not let your hearts be troubled.
Trust in God; trust also in me.

John 14:1

Do not be anxious about anything, but in everything,
by prayer and petition, with thanksgiving,
present your requests to God.

Philippians 4:6

heaven: your future home

And God shall wipe away all tears from their eyes;
and there shall be no more death, neither sorrow,
nor crying, neither shall there be any more pain:
for the former things are passed away.

Revelation 21:4 KJV

Whoever lives and believes in me will never die.

John 11:26

If you have enjoyed this book,
we'd love to hear from you.

Please write:

Book Feedback
Hallmark Cards, Inc.
2501 McGee Street
Mail Drop 215
Kansas City, MO 64108

booknotes@hallmark.com

Look for Gift Books From Hallmark wherever Hallmark cards and other products are sold.